Trump's Autistic Locker Room

Travis Breeding

ISBN: **1540869938**

ISBN-13: **978-1540869937**

DEDICATION

To all affected by autism and mental illness.

CONTENTS

ACKNOWLEDGMENTS

I would like to thank my friends and family for making this a possibility for me.

TRUMP'S AUTISTIC LOCKER ROOM

Now that every teenager I meet with autism

thinks that locker room talk is something that is

okay to do at all times thanks to the President

Elect Donald Trump, I am having a hard time

explaining to kids I meet with autism why they

should not be following their President Elect's

lead on everything that he does or says.

In past presidencies I did not personally agree with everything with every single president but there has never been a president who has been more careless in his campaigning and with the words that he says than Mr. Trump has said.

I really do believe that if the democrats had chosen Bernie Sanders or really any other candidate than Hillary Clinton that the democrats would have beat the republicans in a land slide election and the democrats probably would have won back the house and senate.

That is not the case so now we are left here trying to figure out what Mr. Trump wants to do with our great country. He has been promising for a couple of years to make America great again but I wonder if America can ever really be great again with a leader with such negative morals and values. It is very concerning to me to think that my children might grow up in an era where teenage boys in school think it is okay to talk about women in sexual ways in the locker room and just consider it locker room talk.

It is hard enough for people with autism to know what is and is not appropriate and we spend countless hours trying to teach everyone what is appropriate and what is not but we just never seem to be able to get it all perfect and when we have leadership who talks about people the way

that the republican party is being led right now it

is very alarming to our children. I feel like

everything we teach children is everything that

Mr. Trump is doing wrong.

The people from the republican party accuse the

media of making up stories about Mr. Trump but I

did not have to listen to any media reporting to

hear and see what Mr. Trump is doing. He had

such bad manners at his debates that he seemed

like a little kid. He has no respect for anyone. We

seen that in the way he talked about women in

the video coming off of the airplane and we also

seen it during one of the debates when he called

Mrs. Clinton a nasty women.

I wonder where our country is headed right now but I do not think it is anywhere good. Although I will say in theory, many of the ideas that Mr. Trump as our good ones as long as he can follow through on campaign promises and make sure that these things happen for us.

He wants to build a wall. That would help with immigration and I think that is amazing. He wants to limit spending overseas and take care of our own people again. One thing that makes America so great is that we have always tried to look out for other people. Sometimes in doing so we have done it so much that we have just endangered ourselves and made things worse for ourselves.

If Donald Trump is going to be successful I feel like he must address some of the nasty things that he said to people in our country during his campaign. I think we can all come together but I do think that we would do much better at coming together if when he takes office Mr. Trump addresses the nation and tells everyone what is going on and how he is going to fix America as well as apologizes for some of those mean and nasty things that he has said in the past.

Mr. Trump created so much tension within his own party that he now has to repair relationships within that party. I am anxious to see how Mr.

Trump will address a divided nation that he helped divide even further during his campaigns.

Growing up it was very hard for me to understand what boys my age talked about. In middle school boys started talking about girls and that only got worse the older I got. I was always made fun of by my peers for not understanding what boys my age were supposed to be talking about. I remember the boys laughing at me and hitting me and telling me what a terrible person I was because I did not talk about banging girls or hitting home runs.

In fact, one summer there were boys bragging about hitting home runs over the summer when I was in high school and they asked me how many home runs I had hit. I said five because that is how many home runs at hit in Little League that summer. Apparently those guys were not talking about baseball and they were expressing locker talk like Mr. Trump approves of.

I tried for years to avoid locker room talk because I feel it is disrespectful of women. I know I would not want anyone talking that way about my daughters if I had daughters and I certainly would not want anyone talking about my wife in that way as well.

Mr. Trump needs to realize one thing. He needs to lead by example. If he wants to be president of the free world than he needs to step up and apologize for some of those things he said. I do have a great deal of respect for Mr. Trump running for president and pulling off the biggest upset we can ever remember but I wish he would address some of the very people that he hurt.

I wish Mr. Trump a lot of successes but there are many people that I know of in the disability community who are scared to death what is going to happen to them next year when he gets in office on January 20th, 2017.

I am hopeful Mr. Trump will try to improve disability services instead of hurting them but everything I am reading says that Paul Ryan and Mr. Trump are very anxious to get in and cut

Medicaid and Medicare so I am left wondering what people with disabilities like autism and schizophrenia like myself will end up doing if Trump does make those cuts to the programs.

I would love to get a job and work full time if I could have better support services on staff I feel like I would be able to do that much better but because my service staff is not quite trained very well on autism I am having to work harder to try and teach them how to help me than I am trying the job itself.

As autism advocates and professionals who work with children on the autism spectrum every day we must continue to work hard to make sure all of our kids understand the slang language and everything goes on with it so that they do not get made fun of.

Locker room talk is going to become more and more popular amongst teenagers because we have a president who openly admitted to speaking terms of locker room talk. Mr. Trump talks like every locker room in America talks about women and sex and that simply just is not true at all. I encourage Mr. Trump to visit some of my locker rooms that I am in with teammates in basketball. I have never heard so many bad words and things said about women in my entire locker room career.

No, Mr. Trump, locker room talk is not the norm and we will work hard to make sure that our kids know that you are not the best role model for them even if you are a good president and make America great again.

I feel like the real question American's should be asking themselves right now is "Can Donald Trump make America great again?" Given his behavior I do not think there will ever be a chance America would be great under his leadership but that is just my professional opinion and I am anxious to see if Mr. Trump can bring America together and help us reclaim the land of the free and the home of the brave.

Mr. Trump has had plenty of women accuse him of sexual assault. I am not sure we have ever had a president who was being considered on criminal charges before but I think either way either with Mr. Trump or with Mrs. Clinton we would have likely ended up with a sitting president being under civil and or criminal investigation. I am not sure if any of these claims will lead anywhere but it is certainly something to keep an eye on.

Mr. Trump likes to tweet and make his voice known. Social media is a great outlet for anyone to get their message across. I am very much a fan of Mr. Trump tweeting. I think that's a great way for him to connect with American's especially the

Americans that are younger and cling to social media as a way of life.

I encourage Donald Trump to continue tweeting from the white house. It will be interesting to see if his staff lets him Tweet as much as he does or if they try and limit it and make it so he only tweets every few days. I know Mr. Trump is quickly adjusting to the idea that he will be president of the United States of America in a little over two months and I wish him all of the best.

I just hate to see all of our kids with autism and teenagers with autism get made fun of in gym class because they do not understand locker room talk. Because of Mr. Trump's locker room talk we must now learn how to address locker room talk

and teach it to teenagers with autism. Best

practice therapies have already been doing this

but we have to get the big training down from the

top level down to the bottom level. Even front

line staff making $8.00 per hour really need to

have more understanding on the issue of locker

room talk, social thinking, and social context.

There is so much more to a social skill than just

the adaptive skill itself and we really have to try

and begin to teach children with autism the social

thinking skills they need to go along with their

social skills. The social skill by itself will help but

without the social thinking skills to know how to

use the social skill it is no good. We must work

harder at teaching people with autism some of Michelle Garcia Winner's concepts and then try to teach them right from wrong. Good role model versus bad role model.

The thing is our kids are always faced with so many choices. However, kids on the spectrum are very black and white thinkers which often means their choice is either 100 percent no or 10 percent yes. We must work very hard with people on the autism spectrum to get them to make better in-between choices so that they can continue to be successful socially both in school and on the job in the workforce.

Donald Trump's comments about women are not

acceptable and we must not pretend that it is

okay just because he is our president. Now that

Donald Trump is president elect we must hold him

responsible for his actions and words. We must

be sure that he is ethical and takes care of all

American's, not just the elite and rich. There are

many poor people without jobs and many

disabled people without services that can help

them lead a normal life. We have to get back to

the basics here in America and I believe with the

right guidance and the proper help we will see a

lot more success for people with disabilities and

the poor. I know Donald Trump wants to be

everyone's president so let's give him a chance to

do that. We owe it to him to give him four years

to see how he envisions America.

Four years may seem like a long time and I know people are just flat out mad at politicians but they are the ones who are making decisions. I really hope that Mr. Trump does away with lobbyist in Washington DC because people should not be allowed to persuade politicians with their money.

With that said I will continue my mission of teaching children appropriate locker room conversations and be sure that they all know that Mr. Trumps version of locker talk is not appropriate for them. I wish Mr. Trump well and happiness for his presidency and future.

President elect Donald Trump offended a lot of

people when he was running his campaign and he really hurt their feelings. I wonder if he is really as much of a bully as people say he is or from what I have read over the internet. I am unsure of what to think of Mr. Trump.

Donald Trump made a lot of good campaign promises on things that he would do or things that he said he wanted to do during the campaign. If he is able to make good on those promises then there is a chance that he could be a pretty good president for our country. I am just wondering if Mr. Trump really thinks poorly of people like him like the media says or if he actually likes everyone and will treat everyone equally.

I am well aware of several people in the autism community and the disability community that are flat out scared and wondering how they are going to survive the next four or eight years. I encourage everyone to wait until this actually starts in January to start freaking out because maybe Donald Trump will not be a bad president. There is a chance he could be a good president but I hope that the media was lying and he really does not feel negatively about people that have less money than him or people who are different than he is.

It is always important to remember that the media has a lot to do with how we view things.

Republicans typically think very negatively of the media because they are very liberal and conservatives think the media is always for the democrats but I do not believe that is the case at all.

One thing is for certain there is a lot of gridlock in Washington D.C. and we need someone to get into office up there to do something and make something happen. Anything happening is better than nothing happening at all which is what has been going on for the last sixteen years. I am so tired of seeing people argue and bicker over things. It feels like politicians have no ability to compromise or make decisions for our country.

There are too many career politicians out there and I love one of Trump's campaign promises where he said he wants to put term limits on congress. I am very excited about that to see if the house and senate will pass such a thing even though they are both republican my hunch is that many of them are going to have a hard time with some of Trump's more liberal ideas.

This was a very interesting election. I really was tired of hearing all of the negative ads. It seems like people cannot run a campaign for office without attacking each other and that is something that really scares me. It is so hard for me to understand why people need to be mean to

each other in order to fight for what they believe
in. In my opinion if you have to attack the other
person that just means you do not have a lot of
good things to say about yourself and makes you
look bad.

I was very confused by the locker room talk thing.
I do think that sort of talk exists in younger locker
rooms but I do not believe it exists in professional
sports. Although if Mr. Trump said that then
maybe I am wrong and misjudging the character
of a lot of professional athletes. It is never okay to
talk so negatively about women and their bodies.
I wish Mr. Trump would issue a public apology to
all women that he hurt and offended and I am

very hopeful that he will not be saying or doing

more things to hurt women while he is in office.

We need a president with good morals and

character to lead our nation during this very

difficult time and I wish Mr. Trump all the best of

luck in trying to make our nation come together.

It can be confusing for anyone to try and

understand locker room talk and what it is all

about but as a person with autism I was even

more confused of it.   I was shocked that a person

running for president would be talking about such

things and it really bothered me. I just could not

find enough reasons to vote for either candidate

in this election so I voted third party because I did

not want to be responsible for either of them.

Imagine being a parent of young children.

Imagine trying to explain to your child why you

voted for someone who thinks so negatively of

women and other minorities who are different

than Mr. Trump is himself. It is scary that I could

be a parent one day and have to explain to my son

or daughter why I might have voted for Trump. It

would be especially bad if I had a daughter. I do

not think I could crush her heart by looking at her

in the eye and telling her I voted for someone that

disrespects women as much as Mr. Trump does.

I know that this country needs to unite and get

things together but are we really uniting around

the right leader for our country? That remains to

be seen and many people have a lot of

uncertainty and fear right now over what might

happen to them under a Trump presidency and a

republican congress. I am trying not to think

about it too much and staying positive. I know

that in the end there is really nothing I can do

about it but speak up and say my opinion and

state my concerns. I feel very scared for my life

right now. Some of the things that I have read

and heard that he said about people with

disabilities has me worrying that he might be out

to hurt me and others like me and that is a very

scary feeling to be disabled and have someone

trying to get you. I know that he will not come

and get me but I worry that he may not have my best interest or the interest of people with disabilities in mind when he is making decisions for our country and its people.

This great country was founded on freedom and it feels like they are trying to take some of our freedoms away. I know people are frightened and not sure what to do with their lives now and there is so much panic going on in groups that I see but we must wait and see what Mr. Trump does and how he plans to improve our country. I do believe that deep down he really wants to help our country but I feel like his character will always be in question because of some of the things that he said and did on the campaign trail. People tend to be very judgmental however that did not seem to hurt Trump when being elected president.

I feel that many people were just so tired and sick of career politicians like the Clinton's that they wanted a complete outsider who would help make America great again. That is what Trump stands for and that is what he aims to do and I am very excited to see his plans for making America great again.

I myself have never actually have never actually talked about women in the way Donald Trump does however I have been tempted to by other guys in order to be cool so I do know that locker room talk does exist and happens but does that really make it okay?

I do not think it is every okay to talk about women inappropriately like that. Women have worked too hard and fought so hard for all of the rights that they have and I do believe that they have a right to be treated with respect and not degraded sexually by men.

I experienced a lot of bullying and peer pressure because I would not talk about women like other men wanted me to when I was a teenager and young man in my twenties. My twenties were very hard for me because I was just finding out that I had autism and I had to learn how to live with a social disorder and at the same time other people were demanding I be very social and people demanded I act like a jerk sometimes or participated in the so called locker room talk in order to be accepted and be cool around other guys.

It was never important for me to be cool with other men. The only person I was interested in being cool with was with a woman and that is something that I continue to work on today because I would love to get married and have children one day.

I do think that one day it will happen but if it does not happen I will always be able to say that I treated women with respect and never

participated in this locker room talk that so many

people are talking about.

Donald Trump might be a good president. It is too

early to tell but one thing is for sure. We as a

people need to demand that he treat all people

equal and fair and stop bullying people that are

not like he is. He should be held accountable and

responsible for his behavior as the leader of the

free world. I hope that he does a lot of good

things for America.

T.B. McHatchins

ABOUT THE AUTHOR

I enjoy camping, hiking, backpacking, and traveling. I hope to visit all 50 states one day along with traveling abroad.

I like meeting new people so I go to new restaurants and hot spots throughout the city from time to time. I also have numerous online friends in which I stay in touch with through social

networking sites like Facebook and Twitter.

I am a sports fan. Football and Basketball are my

favorites. I play some recreational sports for fun

only. I root for the IU Hoosiers, Boston Celtics,

Green Bay Packers and Indianapolis Colts.

I have Asperger's which just means I'm Awesome

Trump's Autistic Locker Room

BIBLIOGRAPHY

Autism at the Casino

Travis shares how he made frequent visits to the casino to help him cope with autism. Travis thought he could get rich and pay everyone to like him and not worry about being socially awkward. His frequent trips to the casino only caused him more problems and landed him in a heap of trouble. He developed an addiction and a whole host of other problems from visiting the casino that he copes with.

Travis spent many years thinking getting rich would solve his problem of making friends and allow people to love him for who he was. Little did he know that all he needed to do was love himself and embrace who he was in order to get others to love him. Travis spent years looking for solutions to his problems on the outside when the answer was right in front of him. All he needed to do was improve his self-esteem and learn to like himself for who he was.

Follow along as Travis turns to outside solutions like going to the casino to solve his social issues related to autism. Will Travis finally get the help he needs from counseling and learn to love himself or will the casino get the best of him and cause him to go bankrupt and end up ruining his life? This is an action packed true story of how a man with autism became confused and started looking for solutions to his autism in all of the wrong places.

Trump's Autistic Locker Room

www.ingramcontent.com/pod-product-compliance
Lightning Source LLC
Chambersburg PA
CBHW070234290526
45789CB00004B/1620